Emerging ITO and BPO Markets

IEEE

IEEE⊕ computer society

⊕ CSPress

Press Operating Committee

Chair

James W. Cortada
IBM Institute for Business Value

Board Members

Mark J. Christensen, Independent Consultant

Richard E. (Dick) Fairley, Founder and Principal Associate, Software Engineering Management Associates (SEMA)

Cecilia Metra, Associate Professor of Electronics, University of Bologna

Linda Shafer, former Director, Software Quality Institute, The University of Texas at Austin

Evan Butterfield, Director of Products and Services

Kate Guillemette, Product Development Editor, CS Press

Emerging ITO and BPO Markets

Rural Sourcing and Impact Sourcing

by Mary Lacity, Joseph Rottman, and Erran Carmel

IEEE computer society

CSPress

Page design by Monette Velasco.

ISBN-10: 0-7695-4918-7
ISBN-13: 978-0-7695-4918-7
Computer Society Order Number: P4918

Contents

Introduction

This IEEE ReadyNote explores two niche sourcing markets: rural sourcing and impact sourcing.[1] Rural sourcing is the practice of locating information technology outsourcing (ITO) or business process outsourcing (BPO) delivery centers in low-cost, non-urban areas. Rural sourcing is a *location* strategy. Impact sourcing is the practice of hiring and training marginalized people in ITO or BPO services who normally would have few opportunities for good employment.[2] Impact sourcing is a *social responsibility* strategy. Rural

---

1   This publication is based on new material and, with permission, material previously published in: M. Lacity and L. Willcocks, *Advanced Outsourcing Practice: Rethinking ITO, BPO, and Cloud Services*, Palgrave, 2012; M. Lacity, E. Carmel, and J. Rottman, "Rural Outsourcing: Delivering ITO and BPO Services from Remote Domestic Locations," *Computer*, vol. 44, no. 12, Dec. 2011, pp. 55–62; and M. Lacity, J. Rottman, and S. Khan, "Field of Dreams: Building IT Capabilities in Rural America," *Strategic Outsourcing: An International Journal*, vol. 3, no. 3, 2010, pp. 169–191.
2   *Job Creation Through Building the Field of Impact Sourcing*, working paper, Monitor Group and Rockefeller Foundation, 2011, http://www.rockefellerfoundation.org/news/publications/job-creation-through-building-field; and Lacity and Willcocks, 2012.

sourcing and impact sourcing intersect when marginalized people in rural areas are hired, trained, and employed in ITO or BPO businesses. But not all rural sourcing firms employ marginalized people, and not all impact sourcing happens in rural communities. The relationship between rural sourcing and impact sourcing is depicted in Figure 1 and is populated by case studies from our own research. CrossUSA and Rural Sourcing, Inc. are rural providers that hire educated IT professionals, so they are not considered impact sourcers. Samasource and Matrix Global are impact sourcers because they hire and train marginalized workers, but they operate in peri-urban or urban areas. Cayuse Technologies, Onshore Outsourcing, and Unicor are rural and impact sourcers. In this Ready-Note, we describe the phenomenon of both markets in more detail and compare and contrast experiences, practices, and lessons learned from these case studies.

Rural Sourcing: a location strategy. ITO and BPO service providers are constantly struggling to attract, train, and retain a qualified workforce. Most providers locate their operations in urban centers such as Dallas, New York, Bangalore, Hyderabad, Dalian, Beijing, and Tel Aviv, where a large labor pool exists. But the downsides of these urban locations are high salaries and turnover. Some providers are pursuing a rural location strategy by building ITO and BPO delivery centers in rural areas, away from the major cities currently serving as centers for ITO and BPO.[3] The main idea of rural sourcing is to locate centers in low-cost areas so that employees can be paid lower wages, allowing providers to pass cost savings to clients in the form of lower prices.

US providers with delivery centers in remote, non-urban, low-cost areas include small-but-fast-growing entrepreneurial firms such as CrossUSA and Rural Sourcing, Inc. (RSI) with ITO delivery centers in Eveleth, Minnesota (population 3,865), and Jonesboro, Arkansas (population 55,515). Large global providers, such as IBM and Dell/Perot Systems, have built delivery centers in rural areas including Columbia, Missouri (population 100,733), and Twin Falls, Idaho (population 40,380). We estimated the US ITO "pure-play" rural outsourcing market to be about $200 million in 2011.[4] This estimate was based on the identification of about 20 entrepreneurial rural ITO providers in the US, with average revenues of $10 million per firm. We have no good way to estimate the value of all the work performed in rural-based ITO or BPO delivery centers that are operated by larger providers like IBM or Dell/Perot Systems. It is quite pos-

---

3   Lacity and Willcocks, 2012.
4   Lacity, Carmel, and Rottman, 2011.

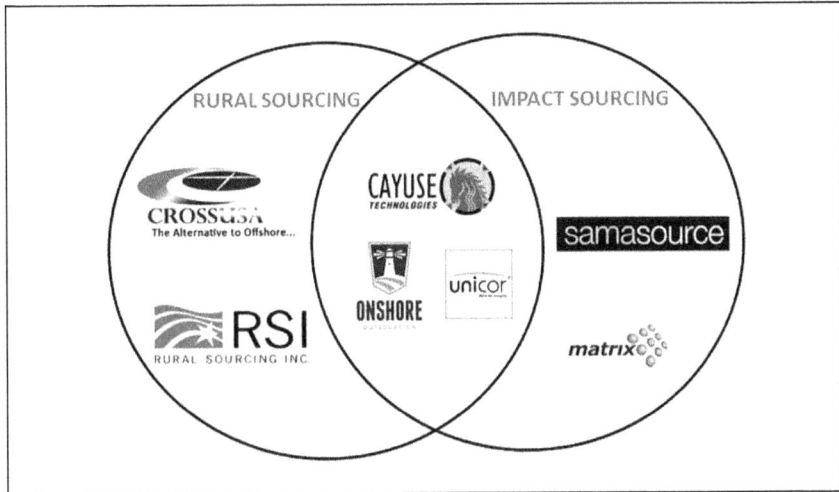

Figure 1. Rural Sourcing and Impact Sourcing

sible that the US rural outsourcing market is worth $1 billion if the value of work from all non-urban ITO and BPO delivery centers were included.

Rural sourcing as a location strategy is a global phenomenon. Providers in many countries are locating delivery centers away from the metropolises currently serving as ITO and BPO hubs.[5] In our 2011 article "Rural Outsourcing," we studied providers in India, China, and Israel that were building delivery centers in rural locations. Consider India: despite the global economic recession, global demand for Indian ITO and BPO services is still very strong and, consequently, Indian providers are still experiencing 14% to 22% turnover in urban areas.[6] By building delivery centers in Tier 3 cities, Indian suppliers lower costs and attrition rates. Chinese providers also cited lower costs, but not necessarily lower attrition rates, by locating in Tier 3 cities. Specifically, they reported that labor

---

5   K. Parakala, "Rural BPOs in India: Are they Over-Hyped?," 2011, http://www.globalservicesmedia.com/Experts/Home/Rural-BPOs-in-India:-Are-they-Over-Hyped/30/27/0/GS110309159353; and M. Zouhali-Worrall, "An Internet for Rural India," CNNMoney, 2009, http://money.cnn.com/2009/07/08/smallbusiness/internet_for_india.fsb/index.htm.

6   J. Arora, "The Risky Side of Offshore Growth: Operational Challenges with Indian Majors?," Everest Research Institute, blog, 25 May 2011, http://www.everestgrp.com/2011-05-the-risky-side-of-offshore-growth-operational-challenges-with-indian-majors-sherpas-in-blue-shirts-4987.html.

costs are up to 50% lower and real estate costs are 70% to 90% lower in Tier 3 cities compared to Tier 1 cities.[7] Because the term "rural" means very different things in different countries (and can even be considered a pejorative term in some cultures), we called this practice remote domestic locations (RDL) when discussing non-US-based providers.

Impact Sourcing: a social responsibility strategy. A 2011 global study supported by the Rockefeller Foundation called "Job Creation Through Building the Field of Impact Sourcing" examines how organizations hire and train marginalized people to perform ITO or BPO work. BPO is seen as offering bigger opportunities for impact sourcing around the world because BPO work requires considerably fewer technical skills than ITO work. The report views impact sourcing broadly; it considers low-employment BPO opportunities in middle- to high-income countries such as the United States, South Africa, Brazil, and Mauritius and urban or rural BPO opportunities in low-income countries such as India, China, Vietnam, Ukraine, and Philippines as impact sourcing. Overall, the report sizes the global impact sourcing market at $4.6 billion in 2010.

The Rockefeller report highlights five case studies of impact sourcing: Samasource, txteagle, Ruralshores, eGramIT, and Digital Divide Data. From these examples, we can also see the overlap between rural sourcing and impact sourcing. Two companies are primarily rural—Ruralshores and eGramIT, both located in rural India. The other three companies have distributed operations covering urban, peri-urban, and rural locations in India, China, Indonesia, Kenya, South Africa, Pakistan, Haiti, Cambodia, and Laos. Two companies are non-profit (Samasource and Digital Divide Data), and three are for-profit (txteagle, Ruralshores, and eGramIT).

Impact sourcing can refer to any organization that seeks to hire and train marginalized people. For the companies and non-profit organizations that create these opportunities, impact sourcing is a social responsibility strategy that provides good jobs for individuals. Such jobs transform not just the individual employees, but also their families and the surrounding communities. We have studied several organizations that hire and train marginalized populations, including Cayuse Technologies in the US that employs Native Americans; Matrix in Israel that employs ultraorthodox "haredi" Jewish women; and Samasource, based in the US, that hires impoverished people living in India, Haiti, Pakistan,

---

7   Lacity, Carmel, and Rottman, 2011.

Kenya, Uganda, and South Africa. We are currently researching another marginalized population, American prisoners. American prisoners are now employed to provide a number of business services that use computer technologies, including call center work, document scanning, and document preparation.

We have been studying providers since 2010, and one message is quite clear: rural sourcing and impact sourcing providers are in a state of constant adaptation. The suite of services offered adapts swiftly to changing client demands, delivery centers open and close, recruitment and training practices change quickly, cultures evolve as companies grow, and providers adjust to environmental disasters like the tornado that left 10,000 people jobless in Joplin, Missouri. These are their stories.

Chapter 1:
Six Providers:
A Brief History and Overview

In this ReadyNote, we focus on six case studies of rural and/or impact sourcing: CrossUSA, Rural Sourcing, Inc. (RSI), Onshore Outsourcing (OO) (formerly Onshore Technology Services), Cayuse Technologies, Matrix, and Samasource. The six case studies are based on interviews and visits to delivery centers operated by five of the six companies (see Appendix A: About This Research). CrossUSA and RSI are rural sourcing but not impact sourcing. Both companies have rural delivery centers, and both companies hire people who have been trained in information technology through a collegiate program and/ or relevant work experience. Onshore Outsourcing and Cayuse Technologies are rural sourcing *and* impact sourcing. Both companies have delivery centers in rural communities, and both primarily pursue an organic workforce development model that trains people for ITO or BPO who otherwise would have no such opportunity. (Both companies also recruit experienced people as well, so the workforce is a mixture of people with and without prior relevant ITO or BPO training/experience.) Matrix and Samasource are impact sourcing but not necessarily rural sourcing. Matrix is an Israeli-based firm that predominantly hires ultraorthodox "haredi" Jewish women. Although Matrix is located outside of the major Israel technology hubs, it cannot be considered "rural" but rather peri-urban. Similarly, Samasource distributes low-level digital work to 16 service providers based in areas of all sizes, including large urban cities (e.g., Nairobi, Kenya, population 3.1 million; Chennai, India, population 8.2 million) as well as small rural communities (e.g., Dharamsala, India, population 19,000).

The six providers vary by location and by organizational age (see Table 1). The US providers are based in different US states: Minnesota, Arkansas, Missouri, Oregon, and California. The oldest company we could identify as a rural provider is CrossUSA, founded in 1998. The newest organization, Samasource, was founded in 2008. Below we describe how each company was founded.

CrossUSA. CrossUSA was founded by Nick Debronsky in 1998. As a businessman, he saw that clients still needed mainframe skills such as COBOL, JCL, ISPF, CICS, and VSAM but that these skills were no longer being taught in universities. He also saw that the people with these skills were increasingly older, isolated, and undervalued. His vision was to aggregate these skills in rural delivery centers. The company primarily hires mid-career employees from all over the country who are looking for a rural lifestyle. The workforce is generally seeking a lifestyle focused on family, good education, and tight-knit, small communities where crime and large city headaches are absent. The corporate office is located in Burnsville, Minnesota (MN), about 10 miles from Minneapolis/St. Paul. The three rural delivery centers were initially located in Sebeka, MN (population 710), Eveleth, MN (population 3,865), and Watford City, North Dakota (ND) (population 1,435). In 2007, CrossUSA closed the delivery center in Watford City because an oil discovery brought an influx of workers that inflated the housing market. CrossUSA successfully relocated 23 of its 30 employees from Watford City to Eveleth. About 60% to 65% of CrossUSA's workload is long-term, full cycle development, and 35% is remote staff augmentation, support, and managed maintenance.[1] The current CEO is Kevin McCloughan. McCloughan was actually a CrossUSA *client* from a Midwestern-based healthcare company before becoming CEO. As of 2011, CrossUSA had nine clients, mostly long-term. The company has 100 employees, generates over $6 million in annual revenue, and is profitable.

---

1   Lacity, Rottman, and Khan, 2010.

Table 1. Overview of Provider Organizations					
Company	**Founded**	**Sales Office**	**2011 Delivery Center Locations**	**Rural Sourcing?**	**Impact Sourcing?**
CrossUSA	1998	Burnsville, Minnesota (MN)	Eveleth, MN; Sebeka, MN	Yes	No
RSI	2003	Atlanta, Georgia (GA)	Jonesboro, AR; Augusta, GA	Yes	No
OO	2005	Macon, Missouri (MO)	Macon, MO; Joplin, MO; St. Louis, MO	Yes	Yes, organic workforce development from rural communities.
Cayuse Technologies	2006	Pendleton, Oregon (OR)	Pendleton, OR	Yes	Yes, the Confederated Tribe of the Umatilla Indian Reservation (CTUIR) created Cayuse Technologies to diversify the local economy and to create living wage jobs that allow the people of the Umatilla Indian Reservation and surrounding rural communities the opportunity to live and work nearby.

Table 1. Overview of Provider Organizations					
Company	Founded	Sales Office	2011 Delivery Center Locations	Rural Sourcing?	Impact Sourcing?
Matrix Global	2004	Modi'in, Israel	Modi'in, Israel	peri-urban	Yes, company hires ultraorthodox "haredi" Jewish women.
Samasource	2008	San Francisco, California (CA)	16 service providers in Haiti, Kenya, India, Cameroon, Zambia, Uganda, Pakistan	urban, peri-urban, and rural	Yes, Samasource aims to end poverty.

Rural Sourcing, Inc. Rural Sourcing, Inc. (RSI) was founded in 2003 by Dr. Kathy Brittain White. Born and raised in Oxford, Arkansas (AR) (population 642), she knew that many students are educated in rural universities but move to urban areas for employment after graduation due to the lack of opportunities in rural America. This phenomenon, called "The Rural America Brain Drain," prompted her to build delivery centers in rural areas anchored by excellent rural universities. She spent a considerable amount of her time and energy building relationships with the universities to establish three delivery centers. She built facilities in Jonesboro, AR (population 59,358, near the University of Arkansas), Greenville, North Carolina (population 84,986, near East Carolina University), and Portales, New Mexico (population 17,000, near Eastern New Mexico State). By 2007, RSI had 75 employees, but the company was losing money and suffered financial losses in 2008. Some of the losses had to do with clients not being able to pay their bills due to the recession. Some of the losses were attributed to poor quality of work, so clients refused to pay. The Greenville and Portales centers closed. By year end, fewer than 20 employees remained. In 2008, Clarkston Consulting bought RSI because it believed in the rural sourcing model. Clarkston has a vibrant ERP business and sought to source some of its client work through RSI. Clarkston gave RSI employees training in ABAP (a programming language in SAP) and implemented quality assurance, project management, and mentoring processes. In January of 2009, Monty Hamilton, a long-time partner at Clarkson, became CEO of RSI.[2] As of 2011, RSI had delivery centers in Jonesboro, Arkansas, and Augusta, Georgia, and employed 100 people. The company is profitable and has had rapid revenue growth: sales were $300,000 in 2008, $1 million in 2009, $3 million in 2010, and between $8 and $9 million in 2011.

Onshore Outsourcing. Onshore Outsourcing (OO) was founded by Shane Mayes in 2005 in Macon, Missouri (MO) (population 5,538). His wife was attending medical school nearby, and there were no job opportunities for him—or other highly skilled knowledge workers—in this small town. He was, what he refers to as, "asymmetrically motivated"; he had no choice but to create his own opportunities for himself and for his newly adopted community. Before moving to rural America, he worked for a large publisher in St. Louis, where he managed globally dispersed IT teams, including 150 people based in India. He knew the value proposition as well as the challenges of offshore outsourcing and thought he could develop a skilled workforce in Macon. His idea was to develop a completely organic workforce by "taking underemployed, dislocated workers who don't have a culture of winning—maybe they are working at McDonald's—and we turn them into software developers." OO focuses training on .NET and Microsoft certifications. OO has delivery centers in Macon and Joplin, MO (population 49,775), and also has staff based in St. Louis, MO.[3] As of 2011, OO had 100 employees, earned about $7 million in annual revenues, and was profitable. In summer 2011, Mayes participated in former US President Bill Clinton's Global Initiative America and pledged to bring 1,000 new jobs to Missouri over the next five years.

Cayuse Technologies. Cayuse Technologies was founded in 2006 and is owned by the Confederated Tribes of the Umatilla Indian Reservation (CTUIR) of the northeast region of Oregon. The idea for the company came from Randy Willis—an Accenture executive and a Lakota tribe member—when he was visiting friends on the reservation. Willis knew that the reservation, with 17% unemployment, needed opportunities for employment beyond the Wildhorse Hotel and Casino. Accenture needed more low-cost domestic delivery centers.

---

2   Lacity, Rottman, and Khan, 2010.
3   Lacity, Rottman, and Khan, 2010.

In 2006, CTUIR and Accenture signed a five-year transitional management agreement—extended for five more years in 2011—in which Accenture agreed to train employees and to provide the technology and management assistance. CTUIR and Cayuse Technologies signed an operating agreement that defines their relationship, establishes a joint Board of Directors, and describes how payments are distributed to the tribe. Cayuse recruited locally and held boot camps to train new hires to perform IT work. They had 25 employees in January of 2007. Cayuse initially launched in a trailer until the tribe built a new delivery center in 2008 in the tribe-owned Coyote Business Park in Pendleton, Oregon. Since its inception, Cayuse Technologies has expanded its services to include BPO work in addition to ITO work. Cayuse primarily serves as a contractor or subcontractor for Accenture. As a contractor for Accenture, about 50 Cayuse employees serve as remote executive assistants to 4,000 Accenture managers. As a subcontractor for Accenture, Cayuse develops software and provides a variety of BPO services for Accenture's clients. As of 2011, Cayuse Technologies employs 280 people, of which 54 are tribe members. The company earns about $14 million in revenue annually and is profitable.

Matrix Global. In Israel's tight labor market, high-tech talent quickly gets tapped by the booming tech sector. Beginning in the late 1990s, Israeli firms began going offshore for cheap labor. Matrix Global was set up during that era as a subsidiary of one of the country's largest IT services firms. But Israeli firms, like their American counterparts, had some sour experiences with offshoring. In response, Matrix Global looked inside the country and became the most prominent of the firms that source from the untapped and inexpensive ultraorthodox "haredi" Jewish women (about 5% of the potential labor pool; 10% if men are included). The Israel-based haredi division was founded in 2004, with its main location in Modi'in housed in modern, well-equipped offices a half-hour drive from the center of Tel Aviv. The other important location is Bet Shemesh, about 10 km south of Modi'in. The division has been quite successful—it grew quickly, reaching 600 women by 2010 and 850 women by 2012. Indeed, Matrix is one of several Israeli firms that began impact sourcing in this unique population. Others include 3base, acquired by a Matrix competitor in 2012.

In the hallways and cubicles of these facilities one sees only women wearing religiously conservative attire of long skirts, long sleeves, and head coverings. As stated on the firm's website:

These highly educated, carefully selected, and meticulously trained women have very strict and specific social and community needs. By satisfying these needs and establishing the development centers in the midst of their religious community, Matrix Global has tapped into a high-quality workforce available in substantial numbers at competitive rates. The homogeneous religious environment of the development centers has enabled the formation of a pool of qualified technical personnel with a high degree of loyalty and professionalism.[4]

Samasource. The CEO and Founder of Samasource, Leila Chirayath Janah, created her non-profit to give dignified, digital work to marginalized people around the world. Samasource uses micro-sourcing (i.e., the outsourcing of small tasks) to employees at the "base of the pyramid" who otherwise would have few employment opportunities. Headquartered in San Francisco, California, the organization distributes work to 16 BPO delivery center partners located in India, Haiti, Pakistan, Kenya, Uganda, and South Africa. Janah's business model is to partner with preexisting remotely located delivery centers. Samasource has developed a proprietary work platform that routes work from the cloud to local delivery centers, where it is completed by employees hired by the delivery center partners. Janah knows that rural employees have a strong work ethic, but that remote partners need Samasource's marketing and account management capabilities to attract and satisfy serious business customers. Samasource provides low-level digital services, such as audio or video transcriptions and digitizing receipts, business cards, land records, books, and archives from both print and handwritten sources. The daily wage of about $5 a day is enough to sustain a rural Indian family and is certainly an attractive price point for business customers.[5]

4   Matrix Global, http://www.matrix-global.net/our-workforc.html.
5   Lacity, Carmel, and Rottman, 2011.

Chapter 2:
How Do Providers Attract, Develop, and Retain Talent?

Each provider in our study has a strategy for recruiting, training, onboarding, and developing employees (see Table 2). Among our cases, four providers primarily recruit locally and use boot camps to train employees (RSI, OO, and Cayuse) or subsidize two-year technical college training (Matrix Global). One provider (CrossUSA) primarily recruits nationally for experienced IT workers and thus does not need an extensive boot camp for training. Samasource relies on partners for workforce development.

CrossUSA's model is challenging because it has to find employees willing to relocate to rural Minnesota. OO and Cayuse, with their organic workforce development strategy, have a challenging recruitment and training model because they primarily take local unskilled, underemployed, unemployed, and/or uneducated people and train them to be ITO or BPO workers. All providers stray from their primary recruiting model as needed. OO and Cayuse also recruit trained ITO and BPO employees, particularly for middle and senior positions. CrossUSA recruits college graduates and younger people from Minnesota. Matrix Global recruits some supervisory labor in secular labor markets of Tel Aviv. Some specific aspects of each provider's workforce development practices are described below. Also, see Appendices B and C to learn more from two CEOs about how rural and impact providers have transformed the lives of employees.

CrossUSA. CrossUSA invests heavily in recruiting because it is primarily looking to relocate mid-career professionals from all over America to rural Minnesota. A Director of Recruiting noted, "We recruit people to a lifestyle change, not a career change." Prospective employees are typically recruited for a specific client account, and thus the applicant must demonstrate detailed business domain as well as technical knowledge. For example, a person hired for a healthcare client might be required to demonstrate knowledge of claims administration and adjudication in addition to the required technology skill set. Applicants must pass online proficiency exams, technical interviews with Tech Leads, background checks, and drug tests. CrossUSA also spends considerable time getting to know the prospective employee and his/her family to ensure a good fit. It does not want to hire people who are not committed to relocation. One red flag, as a Director of Recruiting said, is a "trailing house or trailing spouse." A "trailing house" means that the recruit does not intend to sell his or her home. A "trailing spouse" means that the spouse does not intend to relocate with the recruit. Once relocated with spouses in tow and with prior homes sold, employees are very committed to their clients and to their new rural communities. Although CrossUSA has primarily hired experienced workers, in the past two years it has been actively seeking to diversify its workforce to attract some younger people. In summer 2010, about 10% of employees were under age 35, about 15% were between the ages of 35 and 50, and about 75% were over the age of 50.[1]

---

1   Lacity, Rottman, and Khan, 2010.

Table 2. Developing Human Capital				
Company	**Primary Recruitment Strategy**	**Typical Training**	**Onboarding Process**	**Career Path**
CrossUSA	National recruitment; relocation	Minimal; mostly hiring experienced workers	2- to 4-week onboarding/ orientation program; dedicated mentors	• Junior Developer • Programmer Analyst • Systems Analyst • Senior Systems Analyst • Team Lead
RSI	Local recruitment; primarily college students	Boot camps	Paid and unpaid internships	• Intern • Programmer Analyst I • Programmer Analyst II • Senior Analyst: PM track • Senior Analyst: SME track
OO	Local recruitment; primarily organic workforce development	12-week boot camp taught by OTS employees at a renovated vocational college	3-month internship	• Intern • SE1 • SE2 • SE3 • Project Manager
Cayuse Technologies	Local recruitment; primarily organic workforce development of tribe members and non-tribe members	Onsite training in special training rooms; initially held boot camps to train software developers	4- to 8-week paid boot camps; probationary period for new hire	• Junior Associate • Associate • Senior Associate • Managing Associate • Manager • Senior Manager

Company	Primary Recruitment Strategy	Typical Training	Onboarding Process	Career Path
Matrix Global	Local and regional recruitment; primarily ultraorthodox "haredi" Jewish women	Supports education/ training at technical school	Specialized training through partner training subsidiary	
Samasource	Primarily relies on existing partners and thus does not actively recruit employees; does incubate new development partners			

Table 2. Developing Human Capital

Rural Sourcing, Inc. RSI relies heavily on local universities to provide the talent necessary to staff the projects in the sales pipeline. For example, recruitment for RSI's Jonesboro delivery center is enabled by close connections with faculty and advisors at Arkansas State University (ASU) and Hardin University. In fact, the majority of the current employees in the Jonesboro center are graduates of the CIS program at ASU. According to the Vice President of Client Services, "Our VP of HR has a very close relationship with the faculty at ASU and is reaching out to professors of IS to find out who their leading students are and who is staying in the area." The Director of Operations also sits on the advisory board for ASU and has encouraged ASU to increase the amount of ABAP (the primary programming language of SAP) covered in the curriculum in order to better prepare the students for a potential position at RSI. During the interview process, RSI looks for both basic programming and project management capabilities but also looks closely at the potential for a good cultural fit with RSI. It uses a combination of technical and behavioral interviews to find a good capable resource. According to the Vice President of Client Services, "We are really looking for people who enjoy learning new things and have the ability to stretch their own skills and capabilities." New employees participate in an extensive boot camp, and almost all of the participants who complete it become paid interns who finish the pre-engagement training. Once hired, RSI uses a combination of a relatively high wage, a generous benefits package, a challenging work environment, and significant opportunities for personal advancement to achieve a very high retention rate. In the 18 months prior to our interview, RSI had only one person leave voluntarily and terminated two employees. Additionally, several people had been referred by current employees and hired, thus enhancing the work environment and improving retention.[2] The average age of employees is about 28 years.

Onshore Outsourcing. This company, as previously noted, primarily pursues an organic workforce development strategy. To identify candidates, OO holds local job fairs that typically attract about 100 to 150 people. People interested in OO are asked to take an online aptitude test that assesses a person's logical reasoning skills. Candidates who pass that test are interviewed to assess their attitudes and behaviors. Candidates who pass the behavioral interview qualify for the 12-week boot camp. The boot camp curriculum was developed and is delivered by OO in the wing of a vocational college in Macon, MO, that OO transformed into an IT training center. The company runs about three boot camps per year. The cost of tuition is about $3,500. Students must pass two Microsoft certifications and successfully complete a capstone project before being hired as an intern. Internships last three months, and successful interns are offered positions as an SE1 (Systems Engineer 1). The employees come from quite diverse backgrounds, including young men with no higher education but with an interest in computer games, single women taking care of children or parents, older men who had careers in older technologies, and residents who left for a good education, want to return home, but cannot find work in their chosen fields. According to Mayes, "It isn't easy to turn blue-collar workers into white-collar workers. It's a labor of love."[3]

Cayuse Technologies. Cayuse Technologies aims to offer job opportunities to tribe members as well as to local non-tribe members. In response to a question related to tribal member recruitment, the Business Development Manager said Cayuse seeks to retool tribe members "from brawn to brain jobs… We are pulling people from the wheat fields, off their horses, and giving them full-time employment with health benefits." Cayuse advertises positions in the tribal newsletter, attends local job fairs, and relies on word of mouth to attract recruits. Cayuse does not require recruits to have college degrees. Employees are trained at boot camps that range in duration from four to eight weeks, depending on the type

2   Lacity, Rottman, and Khan, 2010.
3   Lacity, Rottman, and Khan, 2010.

of work the employee will be performing. BPO employees may need very little training prior to being assigned to a project, but highly technical skills such as .NET development and Java require significant training. In addition to technical training, Cayuse also uses Accenture's delivery methodology to improve the employees' communication, relationship building, and public speaking skills. In addition to boot camps, employees can also have tuition reimbursed if they choose to pursue further education. In 2011, Cayuse partnered with Eastern Oregon University (about 50 miles away) to offer college computer programming courses onsite at Cayuse Technologies, taught by Cayuse employees. Eastern Oregon University students and current Cayuse employees may take the courses. Both Eastern Oregon and Cayuse hope that this initiative will pave the way for future Cayuse employment. Career paths at Cayuse are being realigned to create one career path, regardless of whether an employee is performing ITO or BPO work. The new "unified career model" aims to promote an equitable culture among employees and to more easily transfer employees between ITO and BPO service lines. The model comprises the following levels: junior associate, associate, senior associate, managing associate, manager, and senior manager.

Matrix Global. The women who come to work at Matrix are young—at an average age of 23. Matrix offers them employment opportunities where few existed before for them. The women are all high school graduates and have 2+ years of technical school training that is usually subsidized by Matrix. Most live very close to Matrix's offices. Some can walk to work. The COO, herself ultraorthodox, explains: "What we are doing here is bringing employment into [this special] community. It is close to home. The Generation Y of ultraorthodox Israeli women wants a challenging job, but they want to be at home." An employee who illustrates this unusual workforce is the employee of the year for 2011, a 35-year-old mother of ten children, who received the award because she rose to become the team leader in the testing unit. She develops applications in C++ and manages automated testing. The women are loyal to the firm for a number of reasons. One is that it is a good cultural fit for them: "This is a place that was designed for ultraorthodox women," said the COO. Women have 14 weeks of maternity leave and are reported to be eager to return to work once the leave is over. Attrition is "too low" at less than 1%. "We take good care of our employees, and that's why we have such low turnover."

Samasource. Samasource primarily relies on local partners to hire and train employees. The partner companies and their workers are featured on the Samasource website (http://www.samasource.org/impact/). For example, one featured partner is Ken-Tech Data Ltd., based in Nairobi, Kenya. This company employs 100 workers. Ken-Tech Data recruits Kenyan youngsters from economically challenged backgrounds and helps develop their skills both educationally and professionally. Usha Martin Rural Services, based in Jharkhand, India, is another featured partner. Jharkhand is one of the least developed areas of India and has a large tribal population. Usha Martin Rural Services trains and employs youth and women from villages. The company currently employs 37 workers. A third example of a partner is The Woman's Digital League, located in Rawalpindi, Pakistan. This is the first company incubated by Samasource. The company is woman-owned and is operated and staffed by 22 women.

Chapter 3:
Client Perspectives:
The Value Proposition

In this chapter, we provide the client's perspective on rural/impact outsourcing. Based on our US client interviews, rural outsourcing clients can be generally classified into three groups: (1) clients seeking an alternative to expensive domestic models (e.g., hiring part-time contractors or engaging urban-based providers), (2) clients seeking an alternative to frustrating relationships with offshore providers, and (3) clients pressured to perform work onshore. In general, *the value proposition of rural outsourcing is that clients pay lower prices for ITO or BPO services compared to services based in urban areas, and clients receive a better service experience compared to offshore outsourcing.*[1]

---

1   Lacity, Rottman, and Khan, 2010.

17

Price-wise, rural outsourcing offers prices that are 25% to 50% less expensive per hour than urban rates in cities such as New York City, Los Angeles, and Chicago. Compared to offshore outsourcing, hourly rates are more expensive with rural outsourcing. For IT work, rural outsourcers charge blended rates between $40 and $65 per hour for software developers, but the transaction costs are significantly lower compared to offshore outsourcing. Compared to offshore outsourcing, rural outsourcing clients spend less money on travel, coordination, rework, knowledge transfer, and onsite liaisons. Concerning service quality, rural outsourcing promises to offer superior services when compared to offshore outsourcing because of better domain knowledge, greater cultural compatibility, and time zone advantages. Furthermore, the high retention rates in rural outsourcing firms protect knowledge transfer investments. We also heard from clients who wanted to send work offshore because they are satisfied with the prices and service quality, but regulations or end-client preferences/restrictions prevent them from doing so. For example, a healthcare company we spoke with manages benefits for low-income families supported largely by government programs like Medicare. Their IT manager said, "We work for state governments. It's important for them to know where the work is happening. It's a very different conversation to say that work is going to go to St. Louis or rural Missouri than it is to say that work is going to go offshore."

We also asked clients of rural providers (CrossUSA, RSI, OO, and Cayuse), "Is patriotism driving client demand for rural outsourcing?" Our findings suggest the answer is no. US clients are attracted to rural outsourcing because of the value proposition. Although US clients like the idea of employing American workers, they would never do so if another sourcing model offered better financial or business benefits. One client said, "I wasn't going to make a fiduciary mistake just because I like to fly the American flag." Another client said, "No flag waving, no corporate social responsibility—quality is the main concern [for selecting rural outsourcing]." A third client stressed that his company's margins are so tight that he would never pick rural outsourcing just for its political appeal. He said, "Let's be frank, if the price doesn't work, your conversation has ended." The rural providers also agreed. The President of CrossUSA said, "The customer doesn't care that you are rural. The customer cares that you can solve their problems and can offer good value."

However, for some clients, appealing to patriotism helped sell the idea of rural outsourcing to their organizations. One healthcare company provides healthcare to a highly unionized population. The CTO was able to use the rural location of the provider as a selling point to convince his customers that rural outsourcing was preferable to offshore outsourcing. The CTO said,

> That was my selling point here. In 2002, one third of our customers were union—firemen, police, sanitation—and with all the noise around outsourcing and September 11th, my strong selling point was, "Look, I need to be able to lower my costs, I need to meet the demands of the business, I need to help the company be profitable and help our members, and by the way many of our members are union employees. I have a way of doing it that keeps the jobs in the USA." That was a very strong selling point to get the concept funded.

Impact sourcing providers aim to make the world a better place by employing marginalized populations. At OO, founder Shane Mayes aims to give rural people better lives. At Cayuse, tribal leaders aim to diversify their economic base beyond casino gaming, fishing, and agriculture. At Matrix, the founder of the subsidiary aimed to provide good jobs for ultrareligious women who had few opportunities for good employment close to home. At Samasource, founder Leila Chirayath Janah aims to end poverty in the digital age. Impact sourcing providers, however, do not proselytize their social missions to clients; they sell clients good services at a good price. Some clients do prefer to select providers not only for price and service, but also to help meet corporate social responsibility objectives, such as buying a certain amount of services each year from minority-owned businesses. For clients, then, **the overall value proposition of impact outsourcing is: favorable pricing, good services, and meeting corporate social responsibility objectives**. In Table 3, we list the value proposition, services, and sample clients for each provider as found on their websites. After the table, we provide sample client experiences for four providers.

Table 3: Value Proposition, Services, and Clients

	Client Value Proposition from Provider Websites	Services Portfolio	Sample Client List
CrossUSA	• "The alternative to offshoring" • "Rural business model that leverages lower-cost IT resources with high-performance and quality results" • "High-quality, rural lifestyle to our employees and cost savings to our clients"	• Full Life Cycle Application Development • Long-term Staff Augmentation • Application Outsourcing • Enhanced Maintenance	• East Coast Health • Insurance Company • Midwestern Life Insurance Company • Midwest Steel Manufacturer • East Coast Media Firm
RSI	• "Domestic Sourcing as an alternative to offshore outsourcing" • "Low cost of living US-based locations" • "Hiring and training skilled IT professionals" • "Competitively priced with offshore firms" • "Easily expandable and collapsible staffing" • "On-site and off-site resources" • "Experience with Industry Standards and American business practices"	• Business Application Management • Application Design & Development • Integration • Data Migration & Conversions • Quality Assurance & Testing • Comprehensive Project Management	• Clarus Information • BlueCross BlueShield • Seneca Foods • RJ Reynolds • The Rawlings Group

Table 3: Value Proposition, Services, and Clients			
	Client Value Proposition from Provider Websites	**Services Portfolio**	**Sample Client List**
OO	• "Rural outsourcing offers a cost-effective yet risk-averse alternative to offshore outsourcing" • "Ideal for Export Control work" • "100% American-English-speaking" & "Cultural Fit" • "Commitment to Partnership" • "Highly scalable, customizable workforce" • "Cost-Effective" • "Low start-up costs over offshore" • "Simplified engagement model"	• Software Development & Integration Testing • Business Intelligence • Maintenance & Support Consulting	• The State of Missouri • ABB • Classic Air Crafts • MasterCard • Centene • Medical Technologies Group • Missouri University of Science & Technology • Macon Atlanta State Bank
Cayuse	• "Cayuse Technologies' business model provides customer satisfaction by leveraging a well-trained, knowledgeable, and specialized technology workforce."	• Software Development • Customer Contact Center • Business Process Outsourcing • Document Image Processing	• Accenture

Table 3: Value Proposition, Services, and Clients			
	Client Value Proposition from Provider Websites	Services Portfolio	Sample Client List
Matrix Global	• "Deals with offshore and nearshore services in Israel and Eastern Europe." • "High-quality, professional services of software development, manual and automatic software testing, and technical and application support with a great cost/benefit ratio."	• Software Development • Maintenance and Support • QA and Software Testing • Source Code and User Documentation • System Conversion • Data Cleansing	• HP • Texas Instruments • Motorola • Juniper Networks • Major Israeli banks
Samasource	• "Get your work done. Save money. Improve quality." • "Samasource offers high-quality business listing verification, data entry, content moderation, and more—so you can focus on your customers and profits, instead of the busy work."	• Content Moderation • Text-Based Judgments • Transcription • Digitization • Data Entry • Data Mining • Business Listing Verification	• Benetech • Intuit • GoodGuide • LinkedIn

CrossUSA. In 2004, Richard Jones,[2] CTO of a $10 billion healthcare company located in New York City, was paying $90 per hour for domestic contractors to help support his mainframe legacy systems. Besides the high hourly wages, the domestic contractor model had other limitations—high turnover and high transaction costs. According to Jones,

---

2   Client representatives and their firms are assigned pseudonyms to protect their identity.

We had a revolving door of consultants coming into our building and leaving after one project. We would spend a lot of money training these consultants, then they would work on a project, and then they would leave. We were also dealing with many small firms. If I had 30 consultants on site, I was dealing with 10 different firms.

Jones engaged CrossUSA in 2004. Jones initially sourced five people from CrossUSA but now engages over 30 people. He finds the overall value of rural outsourcing to be high in terms of price, quality of work, low turnover, and management of a single provider. He said, "CrossUSA delivers quality work. They take a project from the beginning to the end, through the entire project life cycle. They have become an integral part of our organization."[3]

Rural Sourcing, Inc. In 2008, John Watson, Senior Project Manager at a software company located in Boston, had engaged a provider based in India to build a strategic dashboard for their core data analysis tools. The provider said it would take six months to build. After 18 months, it was still not properly built. Watson said, "They would tell us a bug was fixed, it pops up again three months later, and they want to be paid again to fix the same bug. How many times do you pay the mechanic to fix the car?" Besides the project delays and excessive rework, the offshore sourcing model required Watson to start his workday at 5:00am to conduct calls with the Indian provider. On these calls, Watson said, "All you heard was 'yes, yes, yes,' but by the next meeting they still haven't done it." Watson engaged RSI in June 2009. Currently, six RSI employees are devoted to the account. Watson reports satisfaction similar to Jones' with both the price and quality of service from rural sourcing: "RSI is opposite of the Indian supplier. We tell them give it to us in a month, and they give it to us in a week. They built the 20 platforms in a month that would have taken the Indian company six months."[4]

Onshore Outsourcing. Jones and Watson served as examples of engaging rural outsourcing providers for application support and application development. A Midwestern financial services company serves as an example of outsourcing data analysis to a rural provider. This company receives millions of credit card transactions per day from banks all over the world that must be matched with the merchants. Data matching often requires human intervention, interpretation,

---

3   Lacity, Carmel, and Rottman, 2011.
4   Lacity, Carmel, and Rottman, 2011.

and processing. Data analysts require quite a bit of training on the company's transactions, processes, and data. Sending this work offshore was troublesome because of the high provider employee turnover, which meant multiple cycles of knowledge transfer. The company engaged OO in 2006, and the same analysts still work for them five years later. Thus—for this financial services firm—workforce stability is a significant benefit of rural outsourcing. The client lead said, "It's been a great relationship."

Cayuse Technologies. Cayuse Technologies' main client is Accenture. Where appropriate, Accenture subcontracts to partners such as Cayuse Technologies to obtain good work that costs less than urban-based alternatives. Cayuse has to compete for work along with other Accenture delivery options. In subcontracting engagements, an Accenture Client Lead serves as the interface between Cayuse Technologies and Accenture's client. Accenture's end clients do not typically engage directly with Cayuse Technology employees, except in customer contact center work. One of Cayuse's largest subcontracts is for a 60-seat, Tier 1 call center support with a Fortune 500 company. The client company found that insourcing the call center was too expensive, but that outsourcing to Asia was not a good cultural fit for this work. Cayuse Technologies was selected because call center rates were less than in-house rates and because the service quality was expected to be better than Asian-based providers. Compared to offshore rates, Cayuse is about $15 an hour more expensive than an Indian call center. The Accenture Client Lead for the contact call center subcontract was most pleased with the quality of service. He said,

> We are exceeding all customer satisfaction metrics with Cayuse. I
> just had a meeting with my Vice President and two Executive Di-
> rectors, and I love showing our satisfaction numbers. The call center
> handles 12,000 calls a month, and our numbers are 'off the chart.'
> Most of the responses rate the Cayuse service as 8.5/9.0. That is
> unheard of in a call center. They go the extra steps to follow up with
> clients and make sure the problems are resolved. I don't tell them to
> do that, but I am very happy they do!

Matrix Global. Matrix's clients are domestic organizations including several very large American Multinational Corporations (MNC) with presence in Israel, plus the wealthy Israeli high-tech firms that would otherwise offshore, seeking lower wages. Entry-level pay starts at around $1,000 per month, well below comparable positions in Tel Aviv. Wages also tend to rise more slowly than elsewhere in Israel, allowing Matrix to offer IT services at prices competitive with places like India, Bulgaria, and Ukraine.[5] The COO told us: "Israeli firms are using us instead of going offshore.… The firms keep the high-end activities in-house, and then the lower-level work is either offshored or comes to us." For the buyer, a provider like Matrix offers a multi-faceted value proposition: low cost, ease of doing business, nationalism, corporate social responsibility (CSR), and low turnover.

5   N. Sandler, "Israel's Matrix Taps Devout Women for IT," *BusinessWeek*, 2009, http://www.businessweek.com/globalbiz/content/sep2009/gb20090916_846021.htm.

Chapter 4:
Lessons for Clients

T he clients of CrossUSA, RSI, OO, and Cayuse all report high levels of satisfaction with the quality of services. Beyond their verbal reports, all clients are "repeat customers," which is perhaps the most convincing evidence of client satisfaction with rural/impact sourcing providers. During our research, we identified four lessons for clients seeking to engage such providers.

Lesson 1: For large clients, rural/impact outsourcing will be part of a global sourcing portfolio.[1] Rural outsourcing/impact outsourcing will likely complement many large-sized clients' sourcing portfolios, which include in-house labor (insourcing), strategic partnerships, staff augmentation, urban-based domestic providers, nearshore providers, captive centers, and offshore providers. To understand how rural and impact outsourcing fits into a global sourcing portfolio, see Figure

---

1   Lacity, Carmel, and Rottman, 2011.

2. This figure maps work to the ideal sourcing model based on the ***degree of work complexity*** and the ***degree of business criticality*** and is adapted from our 2011 article in *Computer* magazine.[2] ***Work complexity*** is the degree to which work requires compound steps and highly idiosyncratic knowledge (e.g., high human asset specificity),[3] involves the control of many variables, and/or features subtle and dynamic cause and effect. ***Business criticality*** is the degree to which a client organization views IT or BP work as a critical enabler of business success[4] or the degree to which "failure" to execute the work properly would critically harm the business, such as the potential harm caused by piracy, lost intellectual property,[5] or raising the public's ire in the case of offshoring.[6]

Client organizations frequently use their own employees (insourcing) or engage in strategic partnerships to perform work that is highly complex and highly critical to the business. One US client called this type of work her "blue chip" work. (In poker, tradition has it that the blue chips are the most valuable, followed by the red chips, and lastly the white chips.) Insourcing is appropriate when the client has the skills and resources in-house to execute such work. Strategic partnerships are appropriate for "blue chip" work when clients and providers can identify a mutually beneficial engagement that fosters innovation and trust and when the partners can align incentives and share risks and rewards. Client organizations frequently source work that has medium complexity and medium criticality ("red chip" work) to domestic contractors, to onshore liaisons from offshore providers, to urban-based domestic providers, and, increasingly,

2   Lacity, Carmel, and Rottman, 2011.

3   O. Williamson, "Strategizing, Economizing, and Economic Organization," *Strategic Management Journal*, vol. 12, 1991, pp. 75–94; and O. Williamson, "Comparative Economic Organization: The Analysis of Discrete Structural Alternatives," *Administrative Science Quarterly*, vol. 36, no. 2, 1991, pp. 269–296.

4   J. Teng, M. Cheon, and V. Grover, "Decisions to Outsource Information Systems Functions: Testing a Strategy-Theoretic Discrepancy Model," *Decision Sciences*, vol. 26, no. 1, 1995, pp. 75–103; C. Saunders, M. Gebelt, and Q. Hu, "Achieving success in information systems outsourcing," *California Management Review*, vol. 39, no. 2, 1997, pp. 63–80; and D. Straub, P. Weill, and K. Schwaig, "Strategic Dependence on the IT Resource and Outsourcing: A Test of the Strategic Control Model," *Information Systems Frontiers*, vol. 10, no. 2, 2008, pp. 195–211.

5   M.T. Rao et al., "Trends, Implications, and Responses to Global IT Sourcing: A Field Study," *Journal of Global Information Technology Management*, vol. 9, no. 3, 2006, pp. 5–23; A. Khalfan, "Information security considerations in IS/IT outsourcing projects: a descriptive case study of two sectors," *International Journal of Information Management*, vol. 24, no. 1, 2004, pp. 29–42; and E. Walden, "Intellectual Property Rights and Cannibalization in Information Technology Outsourcing Contracts," *MIS Quarterly*, vol. 29, no. 4, 2005, pp. 699–721.

6   F. Sen and M. Shiel, "From Business Process Outsourcing to Knowledge Process Outsourcing: Some Issues," *Human Systems Management*, vol. 25, 2006, pp. 145–155.

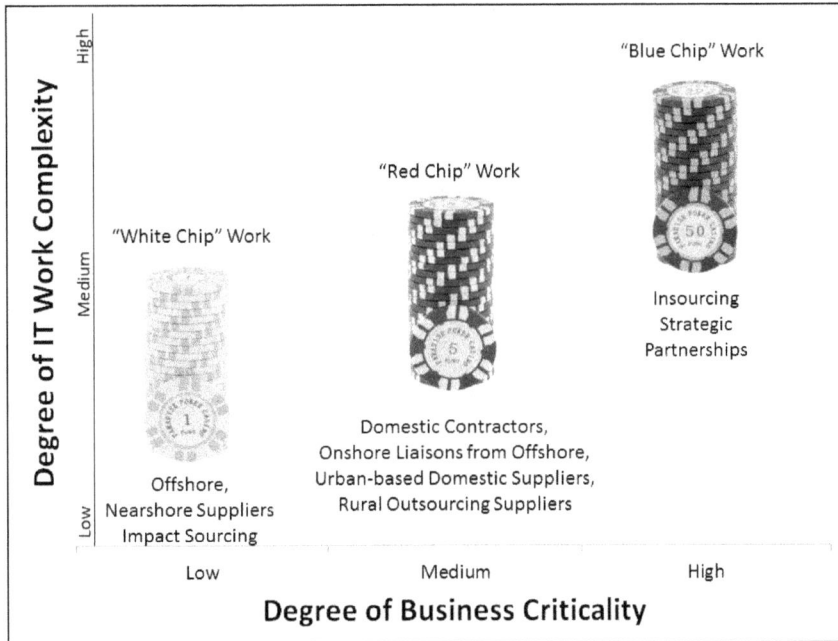

Figure 2. The Portfolio of Sourcing Options

to rural-based providers. For example, a US client engaged Onshore Outsourcing to run legacy systems while her staff focuses on work that is highly complex and highly critical to the business. Client organizations find that the easiest work to send offshore are the so-called "white chips"—the work that is low in complexity (so that it can be packaged, priced, and shipped offshore), and the work that is not critical to the business yet, such as new software that is not yet "live." Clients with a strong sense of corporate social responsibility might also consider impact sourcing, particularly for very low-level, micro-work. Of course, the global sourcing portfolio depicted in Figure 2 captures generalizations. We certainly have studied exceptions, such as client firms sourcing innovation offshore[7] and client firms performing low complexity and low business criticality tasks in-house.[8]

---

7   J. Rottman, "Successful Knowledge Transfer Within Offshore Supplier Networks: A Case Study Exploring Social Capital In Strategic Alliances," *Journal of Information Technology*, vol. 23, 2008, pp. 31–43.

8   R. Hirschheim and M. Lacity, "Information Technology Insourcing: Myths and Realities," *Communications of the ACM*, vol. 43, no. 2, 2000, pp. 99–108.

Lesson 2: Engagements evolve over time.[9] Clients from CrossUSA, RSI, and OO primarily began their engagements on a small scale using a remote staff augmentation model. At first, these clients managed the provider's employees, typically as part of a client-directed project team. Clients started their engagements with as few as two provider employees. Initial tasks were typically part-cycle development (such as coding or testing) or partial maintenance of existing systems, again under close client supervision. Over time, many clients added more people from the providers, extended services to more complex work, and even evolved some engagements into managed services (see Figure 3).[10]

The largest client engagements we studied were also the longest engagements we studied. One US financial services firm grew from six rural sourcing employees in 2006 to 30 people in 2010. They also moved from a staff augmentation model in 2006 to managed services within the last few years. A US east coast healthcare company started with five people in 2004 and grew to 31 people in 2010. The CTO talked about the evolution of the relationship:

> Initially, the model really was remote staff augmentation. We now allow them to work directly with our business where initially we were cautious about that because we did not know if this concept was going to work or not. We have moved away from staff augmentation. The [rural supplier's] systems analysts actually now directly communicate with our business people. Now if we have a project, it is very common to assign a [rural supplier] systems analyst as the project lead. That systems analyst is working remotely, or they deal with business leaders using video conferencing.

Lesson 3: Clients need to plan ahead. The US clients we learned from all report high levels of satisfaction with rural outsourcing in terms of price, quality of service, stability of the workforce, and the political appeal of the model. Clients were driven to rural outsourcing because of the lower costs compared to urban-based domestic providers or because rural outsourcing providers were easier to engage than offshore-based providers. However, there were struggles along the way. The one consistent complaint we heard about rural outsourcing was, "I wish the rural outsourcing provider could scale up faster." For example, one client said he

---

9   Lacity, Carmel, and Rottman, 2011.

10   Figure 3 originally appeared in Lacity, Carmel, and Rottman, 2011.

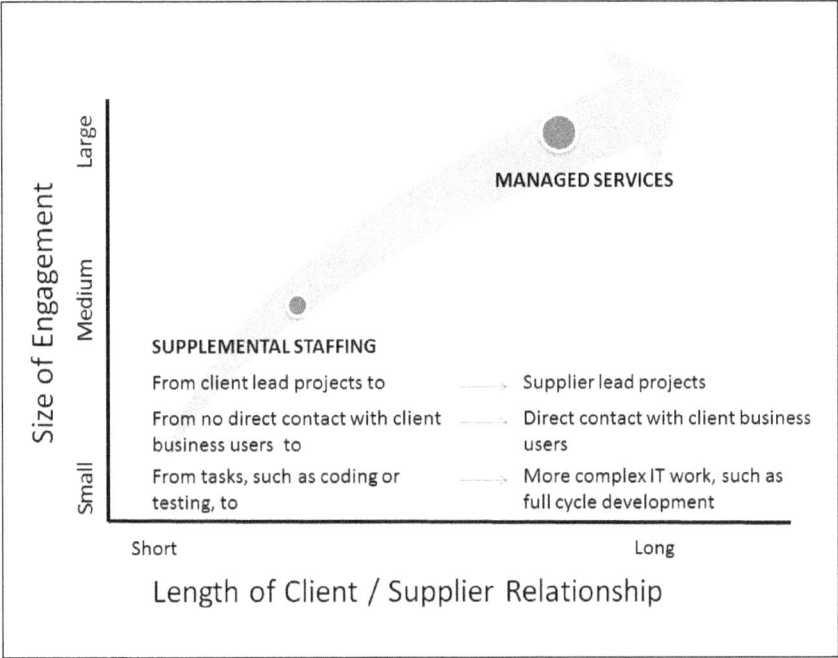

Figure 3. Evolution of Client Engagements

wanted to engage 50 people from his rural sourcing provider, but the provider only had six people with the required technical knowledge and business domain experience. Unlike Indian providers who can staff hundreds of people quickly because of their deep benches, rural outsourcing providers often recruit for a specific client, which can take months. Subsequently, US clients work with rural providers to plan well in advance for workforce needs.[11]

Lesson 4: Clients must invest in the relationship.[12] Most clients also noted that they need to invest in the relationship with the providers, particularly knowledge transfer, to ensure success. When work has middle- to high-complexity, the client organization must properly transfer knowledge to the provider through training, shadowing, and mentoring. At a US Midwestern legal firm, the IT manager did "man-to-man" marking. He said,

---

11 Lacity, Rottman, and Khan, 2010.
12 Lacity, Carmel, and Rottman, 2011.

It is still true that you get what you pay for. If you need a rock star, you're going to have to pay for a rock star. You're probably not going to get a rock star at rural outsourcing prices, so pair the [rural outsourcing employees] up with one of your own rock stars, so a lesser-skilled person from the [rural outsourcer] can absorb and learn quickly and be able to do higher-level tasks quickly.[13]

Another key message we heard over and over again was the need to frequently and meaningfully communicate and interact with providers. For applications development projects, daily calls from the client site to the remote delivery site are the norm. For applications support, weekly meetings are scheduled, and ad hoc voice and video calls are common. For team building, clients also visit the rural delivery centers and invite the rural employees to visit the client site. For example, the US Midwestern financial services firm mentioned above brings the remote employees to their site twice a year, not only for face-to-face meetings, but for social activities like picnics. The CTO from the US east coast healthcare firm described how his visits to the rural delivery center affect the staff:

Just like you have to make an investment in an employee, like investing in their training, making them part of your organization and culture, we realized quickly that we would have to treat these remote people from [the rural outsourcer] just like we would treat our employees. I went to visit them. I spoke to all of their employees like I would speak to my employees when I conduct town hall meetings. My job is to make them feel that they are part of our organization. That is very important for retention of these resources.

---

13   Lacity, Carmel, and Rottman, 2011.

Chapter 5:
Lessons for Providers

The four rural providers profiled—CrossUSA, RSI, OO, and Cayuse—are all successful enterprises as evidenced by rising revenues, profitability, low turnover, and satisfied and repeat customers. As more providers consider establishing rural sourcing centers, they may well benefit from the experiences of these companies.

Lesson 1: Adapt or perish. US-based rural/impact sourcing providers need to be incredibly nimble to adapt to changes in the external environment, like conditions that erode a location's advantage or shifting client needs that require providers to alter their service portfolio. Concerning the former, three providers have closed delivery centers in Portales, New Mexico; Greenville, North Carolina; Watford City, North Dakota; and Lebanon, Missouri. Concerning the latter, CrossUSA expanded services beyond mainframe technologies, OO moved more work from application development to application support, and Cayuse Technologies moved more work from application development to business processes. Shane Mayes, CEO of OO, says it best:

> Everything we did up to now was exactly the right thing we needed to do to get here, but may be exactly the wrong thing we need to do to move forward. Everything I say is gospel as of today, but by tomorrow everything could change.

See Appendices B and C to learn more from two CEOs about how rural and impact providers have adapted their business services in reaction to their customers' needs.

Lesson 2: Location, location, location. With rural sourcing, providers consider a number of factors when choosing the locations of their delivery centers, including the cost of living, the ability to hire and retain a qualified workforce, and support from local governments, regional economic development groups, and academic institutions. These criteria are in conflict. For example, the cost of living criterion is at considerable odds with the ability to hire a qualified workforce. In general, the lower the cost of living, the smaller the hiring pool population. Overall, it is easier to recruit in areas with larger populations but harder to retain employees, as they have more opportunities to change companies. Turnover is a serious consideration for providers because of the considerable investment they make in training new hires. In Table 4, we map the Cost of Living Index with city and county populations for some delivery centers in our case studies and for some large cities and counties. The county populations give a good idea of the resource pool available to providers. For example, CrossUSA's delivery center in Eveleth, MN, is located in one of the cities with the smallest population, but Eveleth is in a county that includes nearly 200,000 people.

One common theme across providers is that the availability of physical facilities is not a primary criterion for location selection. Every provider said that facilities are easy to acquire because so many rural communities have large, abandoned manufacturing facilities that can be easily refurbished with technology. For example, Nick Debronsky of CrossUSA bought and refurbished a carpet factory, and Shane Mayes of OO refurbished a sewing machine factory. RSI spent the first years of its operation in a facility supported by the University of Arkansas. In summer 2010, it outgrew the space and refurbished property in downtown Jonesboro.

Table 4. City Population, County Population, and Cost of Living Index*			
City	Population	County Population	Cost of Living Index
Sebeka	710	13,269	73.6
Eveleth	3,865	197,767	76.0
Macon	5,538	15,359	76.4
Joplin	50,208	118,179	77.3
Lebanon	12,155	35,432	77.7
Pendleton	4,406	75,889	82.8
Jonesboro	55,515	95,457	82.9
Augusta	136,381	539,154	90.2
St. Louis	319,294	1,016,301	90.4
Ann Arbor	112,852	347,563	96.4
Tel Aviv	403,700	3,206,400 (metro)	24th most expensive city in world
Chicago	2,695,598	5,376,837	116.8
Los Angeles	3,792,621	9,519,331	136.2
New York City	8,175,133	19,465,197 (metro)	216.4
* *The average US city Cost of Living Index is 100; numbers below 100 have lower than average living costs.*			

In contrast to rural sourcing, impact providers seek to erect delivery centers in the communities within their target populations, even though other criteria may not be favorable. Clearly, Cayuse was to be built on the Native American reservation. OO was to be built in the founder's hometown community. Samasource partners with organizations located in the most impoverished locations.

Lesson 3: Consider government economic development support. The providers we studied have different views on seeking city, state, and federal government support. On the one hand, a CEO told us, "I wasn't going to build a business by waiting around for a government check." On the other hand, several CEOs benefited from On-the-Job Training (OJT) funds, Community Development Block Grants, and/or property tax waivers or abatements. For example, Shane Mayes, CEO of Onshore Outsourcing, described, in sequence, all of the funding his company received and how it was helpful at key moments:

1. Local revolving loan fund from Macon, Missouri, and the Mark Twain Regional Council of Government provided start-up financing totaling $100,000.
2. Missouri Customized Training Grant was instrumental in the beginning to offset some training costs. The program has been useful throughout OO's history.
3. On-the-Job Training (OJT) funds have been used in the past to offset on-the-job training expenses.
4. A Community Development Block Grant (CDBG) grant was instrumental in helping OO establish our initial workforce development program.
5. A CDBG grant and a loan from Joplin's Revolving Loan Fund were instrumental in establishing an office in Joplin, Missouri.
6. In summer 2012, OO was looking to partner with a University to apply for a grant to add new curricula and enhance the distance learning platform.

For RSI, the most important sources of support have been non-monetary. Monty Hamilton, CEO of RSI, explained,

> First, the local universities and colleges surrounding each of our development centers have been great partners. They are willing to listen to our needs, adapt programs as needed, and serve as a critical component to our supply side for engineers and software developers. Secondly, the local elected and non-elected leaders have been outstanding in their continued support. I'll give you a quick example. We had a senior executive from a Fortune 100 company coming to one of our development centers to understand how we would provide a solution, see our facility, and meet our colleagues. After securing the date on the calendar, I called the Mayor's office to see if he might find a few minutes to say hello to our very important guest. Before I could finish asking for my favor, he not only offered to meet our client but also arranged for us all to have lunch. That kind of support after you've chosen a location makes you feel great about the selection and speaks volumes to our clients about our community support.

There is no denying that government incentives can help launch a new business and help train workers. To get a better understanding of the role of government incentives, see Appendix D, where we asked Christopher Chung, CEO of the Missouri Partnership, to describe incentives and provide examples of how they work.

Lesson 4: Let employees help build the culture. Many large-sized, urban-based providers have a culture that places the client as the top priority. This creates a culture where employees are expected to show the initiative to do everything to satisfy a client by working shifts that match the client's time zone, by working long days to meet deadlines, or by taking extended trips to client sites. Employees trained in the IT profession certainly know and expect such a culture. At some rural or impact providers, however, this type of culture is completely foreign to the local population and creates work-family conflicts that can interfere with the employees' ability to do good work. Some cultures also have very different concepts of "hard work." In tribal, agricultural and fishing cultures, people typically work excessively hard for several months, followed by several months off work. This work culture is different than the work culture needed in an ITO or BPO business. So how can rural and impact providers create a culture focused on clients while also empowering employees? Let employees help build the culture. Consider how this approach helped Cayuse to be successful.

Because Cayuse Technologies had a management contract with Accenture, Accenture quite naturally replicated their processes—from training to supervising—onto the new firm when the company first started in 2006. As Accenture's Executive Director noted, "At first we almost regurgitated the Accenture culture onto the tribe, which didn't work." Accenture had to learn how to deal with the differences between urban and rural workforces and between tribal and non-tribal cultures. Many people in the tribe are single parents who want and need to work, but have difficulty managing a full-time job. Absenteeism was a problem. In urban areas, single parents have resources such as day care facilities and public transportation that ease their home lives so they can be productive at work. So Cayuse management began to question: "How can we help you get your home life in order so you can come to work? Do you need a ride to work?" In 2007, Cayuse managers and employees rebuilt the culture from scratch. The employees identified a new set of core values: diversity, harmonious heart, integrity, quality, teamwork, family, and work ethic. The employees created artwork to go with each value and signed their names. This art is displayed along the main hall of the delivery center. Employees are keepers of the culture and nominate and award annually their peers who best display each value. Attendance is acknowledged and rewarded and has significantly improved. The attrition rate dropped significantly, to about 8% in 2011, which is low turnover for BPO work. Cayuse management continues to experiment with new practices, such as creating part-time positions. So far, four part-time employees have been hired.

Lesson 5: Bring potential clients to the delivery centers. An old adage says that people evaluate what they hear based on who is saying it. Potential clients are skeptical

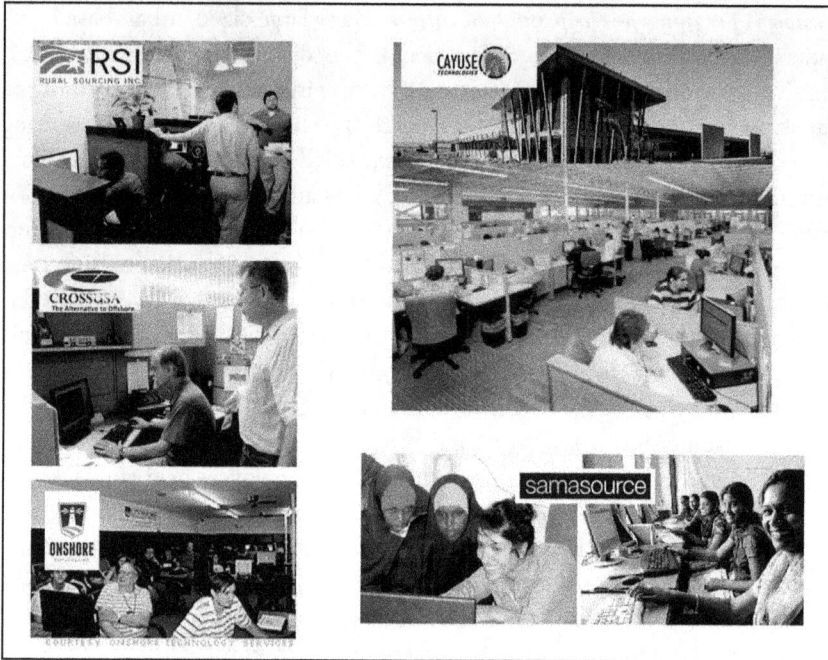

Figure 4. Rural Delivery Centers

of sales people, business developers, and other provider senior executives. Serious potential clients want to meet two stakeholders: the employees who will be delivering the work and current clients. Clients who actually visited the delivery centers were much more likely to engage the provider because they felt more confident in the workforce and in the level of security at the delivery centers. (The same holds true for researchers, as our assessment of the credibility in the rural sourcing and impact sourcing models increased significantly after visiting delivery centers—see Figure 4—and interviewing clients.)

Lesson 6: Create a rural sourcing advocacy group. As an emerging market, the rural sourcing providers we studied are all tackling the same issues, such as educating the client market about rural sourcing, explaining ITO and BPO opportunities to potential employees living in rural communities, and advocating for favorable legislation. For example, a provider said that the client's procurement team has to be sold on the concept of rural outsourcing: "You would think rural sourcing would be an easy sell, but to some procurement teams, it's not an easy sell because it's different from the incumbent solution." Concerning legal issues, some foreign providers with no corporate office presence in the US do not pay prevailing wages when they send employees to work in the United States, creating an uneven playing field. For example, one rural provider bid $50 per hour for development work, only to lose the bid to an Indian provider who could bring work onshore for $20 per hour. The American provider decided to work with its state's Senators to investigate this issue. We believe that rural providers would benefit from their own formal advocacy group. Currently, there are some informal groups, such as the USA OnShoring & Outsourcing Group on LinkedIn. Participation in prestigious organizations, such as the rural subgroup from Clinton's Global Initiative America, is advantageous, but not focused specifically on ITO and BPO work. A formal, industry-specific rural sourcing advocacy group might be modeled after The National Association of Software and Services Companies (NASSCOM), considered to be a critical success factor for India's $60 billion ITO and BPO industry. Perhaps it is indeed time for a RASSCOM.

Chapter 6:
Other Cases of Rural and Impact Sourcing

Thus far, we have focused on six providers and the client and provider lessons we learned from them. Our research on rural and impact sourcing continues, and here we present some additional case studies of organizations we are just beginning to investigate. Our research is global in scale, as sourcing in rural/remote domestic locations (RDL) and impact sourcing are occurring on all inhabited continents. Below we present a view on RDL and impact sourcing in India and China. We also discuss impact sourcing for arguably the most marginalized population of all—US prisoners.

India: Two types of RDL providers. The Indian government and private sector have made significant investments to bring the Internet and training to India's rural

population of 700 million people. For example, Comat, a private-public partnership, opened 800 delivery centers across India and provides English classes and
IT training to the rural population.[1] The workforce in rural India generally has
very low skill levels, but is composed of hard workers who welcome opportunities for employment. We studied two types of Indian providers: for-profit firms
seeking lower costs and a more stable workforce and non-profit organizations
with a social mission to bring jobs to underprivileged populations in rural India.

For the for-profit Indian providers, RDL refers to the practice of building delivery centers outside of the larger cities (such as Bangalore, Mumbai, Chennai,
and Hyderabad, which are labeled Tier 1 cities in Indian business parlance). The
practice, driven by the need for firms to access lower labor costs and to increase
employee retention, began in India in roughly 2006.[2] We interviewed managers
from two such firms: HOV Services, a global provider with 12,000 employees
spread across North America, India, and China, and Zensar Technologies Lim-
ited, an Indian global software and services firm with 6,230 employees across
the globe. Both firms built delivery centers in Tier 3 cities to avoid the high attrition rates prevalent in Tier 1 cities. These attrition rates—which range from
20% to as high as 100%[3]—increase knowledge transfer and transaction costs.
According to Marc Baines of HOV Services,

> When we target the smaller cities, we have much lower turnover
> and are experiencing an increase in the tenure of our employees.
> For example, the turnover in our smaller cities is practically zero.
> This lowers our training costs, increases retention, and allows our
> employees a better quality of life, since they can remain closer to
> their families. We have much better luck in the less developed cities.
> We can pass these improvements directly on to our customers.

Zensar Technologies reports similar improvements in their workforce retention
in Tier 3 cities.

The Indian providers say that workforce development is their major challenge. According to Ravi Ramathan, Global Marketing Controller at Zensar,
"The availability of required skill sets is pretty low, and only certain types of proj-

---

1 Zouhali-Worrall, 2009.
2 Zouhali-Worrall, 2009; and Parakala, 2011.
3 M. Lacity and J. Rottman, *Offshore Outsourcing of IT Work*, Palgrave, 2008.

ects can be executed from these cities." To overcome these challenges, Zensar has begun to enhance the education of the available resources with significant training to prepare workers for employment. For some providers, English language training is also a requirement in addition to IT or BP training.

The other type of providers—those with a strong social mission—are using micro-sourcing (i.e., the outsourcing of small tasks) to employ underprivileged people. Samasource, Desicrew Solutions, Villageshores, and Ruralshores are sample providers in this space.

China: Developing capabilities in Tier 3 cities. "Rural" is not a culturally appropriate term for Chinese providers. The term "rural" connotes economically disadvantaged and/or less-civilized areas within China. Truly rural areas in China do not have the capabilities (e.g., infrastructure, human resources) to support the provision of outsourced services. Therefore, as in the Indian case, we define RDL in China as involving Tier 3 cities. These cities range in population from several hundred thousand to several million. They have sufficient broadband. The RDL firms work on IT service projects for clients from Tier 1 cities such as Beijing, Shanghai, Shenzhen, and Dalian as well as Tier 2 cities such as Chengdu, Xi'an, and Wuhan. RDL employees also work on local projects in their own regions and provinces.

For the three RDL providers we interviewed, cost is their primary advantage. According to them, labor costs for the IT workforce are roughly 50% lower in Tier 3 cities than in Tier 1 cities. Real estate costs in Tier 3 cities are 70% to 90% lower than Tier 1 cities. Moreover, there is some government support: some cities in China still have rent waivers for IT services firms. Some companies actually benefit from the "gray area" of lack of tax regulation in "rural" China. One of the interviewees specifically told us that employees don't have to pay taxes.

For all three RDL providers in our Chinese sample, workforce development was their biggest challenge. In China, there are rather large cities with no local colleges—no source of skilled labor. The president of a firm in one of these cities said that recruiting employees is his "biggest headache" and it keeps him "sleepless at night." Yet, some of the companies are in cities with regional colleges that have graduates in computer science and software engineering. However, all of our interviewees stressed that the college graduates still lack practical technical skills and client readiness. Therefore, some of the remote firms would still prefer to hire experienced employees from the big cities even though they cost at least 50% more. Unlike the three other nations in this chapter, turnover is a problem for the Chinese providers. Trained IT employees are lured by the bigger cities.

Prison Sourcing. Perhaps no other workforce is more marginalized than incarcerated individuals. Able-bodied and able-minded prisoners have always worked—at least in the United States—to defray the costs of corrections and to meaningfully occupy prisoners. Most prisoners, after all, will one day be released. Research on both federal and state prison industry employment programs have found that prisoner work participation is associated with lower recidivism rates, higher rates of employment in halfway houses, and higher wages after release compared to prisoners who were not in these programs.[4] Most prison employment programs train workers in manual tasks, such as furniture building or textiles. But with the advent of the Internet, some prison employment programs now train prisoners to perform low-level BPO services like call center work. For example, the Federal Correctional Institution (FCI) in Elkton, Ohio, has 450 computers in a center on the prison compound where trained prisoners provide business services to external customers. Another example is the all-female state prison at the Arizona State Prison Complex in Perryville, Arizona. This site serves as an example of a private sector partnership. Televerde, the private sector partner, operates four call centers at the complex, and external customers include Cisco, Hitachi, and SAP.[5]

At US federal prisons, the work is managed by Federal Prison Industries (FPI), also known as UNICOR, a wholly-owned government corporation (public partnership) established in 1934. Traditionally, FPI has employed prisoners to perform manual work, such as recycling, furniture making, garment manufacturing, and electronic subassemblies. FPI now sells about $35 million per year in business services, including call centers, capture and conversion for Electronic Document Management Systems, document preparation, and GIS (Geographic Information Systems) and CAD (Computer Aided Design) applications. At state prisons, the Private Sector/Prison Industry Enhancement Certification (PIE) program established in 1979 authorizes state prisons and units of local government to establish partnerships with the private sector for inmate employment. A number of these partnerships offer call center services, including state

---

4   N. Conan, "Inmates' Jobs, From Call Centers to Paint Mixing," *Talk of the Nation*, National Public Radio, broadcast, 16 Dec. 2010; N. James, *Federal Prison Industries (RL32380)*, Congressional Research Service, 2007, http://digitalcommons.ilr.cornell.edu/key_workplace/309/; W. Saylor and G. Gaes, "Training Inmates through industry work participation and vocational and apprenticeship instruction," *Corrections Management Quarterly*, vol. 1, no. 2, 1997, pp. 32–43; and W. Saylor and G. Gaes, "The Differential Effect of Industries and Vocational Training on Post Release Outcomes for Ethnic and Racial Groups," *Corrections Management Quarterly*, vol. 5, no. 4, 2001, pp. 17–24.

5   V. Barret, "Silicon Valley's Prison Call Center," *Forbes*, 28 June 2010.

prisons in Arizona, Oregon, Michigan, New York, and South Carolina. These business jobs can pay about $7.25 per hour, compared to manual labor rates that can be as low as $.25 per hour.[6]

Despite the positive effects of prison industry employment programs on prisoners, the public and private sector partners in these programs have come under attack. Opponents argue that prison industry programs hurt small businesses and steal jobs from law-abiding citizens.[7] For example, a number of actions have been taken against UNICOR for unfair competition, particularly by apparel and furniture manufacturers. In 2003, UNICOR responded by adopting resolutions to raise the threshold of mandatory use by the Federal government of UNICOR from $25 to $2,500 and by granting waivers on all cases where the private sector provides a lower cost. In reality, prison industry employment programs are too small to significantly affect the American economy. Only .00056 percent of the national civilian work force consists of inmate labor;[8] about 15,000 prisoners were employed by UNICOR in 2010.[9] Much of the opposition to prison industry employment programs "has centered around emotional responses to the issue, rather than factual evidence."[10] Since 2004, prison industry programs have addressed this opposition by positioning their business services as keeping American jobs onshore rather than shipping more American white collar jobs offshore.[11] For example, the UNICOR Services Business Group published a brochure on call centers that states, "Recently, UNICOR has been authorized to partner with private sector firms currently sending work offshore or in lieu of sending work offshore."

---

6   Barret, 2010.

7   D. Carroll, "Behind the Fences: UNICOR's Affect on Private Business," *Business Credit*, vol. 112, no. 3, Mar. 2010, pp. 12–13; A. Gruber, "Competing with Inmates," *Government Executive*, vol. 37, no. 12, 2005, pp. 32–34; G. Smith-Ingley and M. Cochran, "Ruinous or Fair Competition: The Correctional Industries Public Debate," *Corrections Today*, Oct. 1999, pp. 82–100; and James, 2007.

8   Smith-Ingley and Cochran, 1999.

9   UNICOR annual report, 2010, http://www.unicor.gov/information/publications/showpub.cfm?pubid=279.

10   Smith-Ingley and Cochran, 1999, p. 98.

11   A. Kramer, "Companies Take Call Centers to Prisons Rather than Overseas," *InformationWeek*, 24 Feb. 2004, http://www.informationweek.com/companies-take-call-centers-to-prisons-r/18200370.

Conclusion

Within the context of the overall global ITO and BPO markets, outsourcing to rural and impact providers, like the previous innovations in sourcing (outsourcing, offshoring, nearshoring, etc.), adds to the menu of choices available in the ITO and BPO industries. Client sourcing needs vary based on the degree of work complexity and the degree of business criticality. Impact sourcing generally finds its place on the low end of the complexity and criticality continuums. Rural sourcing generally finds its place mid-range along the continuum of sourcing options and seems best suited for work with mid-range complexity and mid-range criticality to the client's business.

Although rural and impact sourcing markets are currently small, we are seeing tremendous interest from clients. Clients we interviewed want rural sourcing providers to scale faster because of the favorable value proposition. Overall, US clients reported favorable experiences with their rural/impact providers. Client satisfaction stems from lower prices compared to urban rates, ease of doing business and lower turnover rates compared to offshore outsourcing, and, in some cases, meeting corporate social responsibility objectives. Research shows that clients increasingly are assessing providers based on demonstrated corporate social responsibility.[1]

Scalability is the main complaint from clients. US providers will point to the fact that of the 300 million people living in the United States, about 60 million live in non-urban areas, and thus rural sourcing is highly scalable. Entrepreneurs have quite ambitious goals for growth. For example, Shane Mayes of OO envisions growing his company to $1 billion in revenues with 10,000 people. "I want to build a hundred-year-old business." Monty Hamilton has frequently said his long-term goal is to build RSI to 3,000 people. CrossUSA envisions that it could grow to a $30 to $50 million company. Juxtaposed with the long-term goals, these providers actually scale operations in reasoned measure. Start-up enterprises struggle with cash flow, and most rural providers cannot afford to have a deep bench of non-billable human resources. Instead, growth for providers is in the sequence "sell then build." This is particularly challenging for the leadership team, as they constantly struggle to balance supply of employees with demand from new clients.

---

1   R. Babin and B. Nicholson, "Corporate Social and Environmental Responsibility and Global IT Outsourcing," *MIS Quarterly Executive*, vol. 8, no. 4, 2009.

Appendix A:
About the Research

Since 1989, we have studied many types of ITO and BPO sourcing options, including domestic outsourcing, offshore outsourcing to India and China, nearshoring, netsourcing (cloud computing), microsourcing, and global outsourcing.[1] RDL, or rural outsourcing, and impact sourcing are our newest areas of research. Thus far, we have conducted 62 interviews with rural/impact

---

1   E. Carmel and P. Abbot, "Why Nearshore Means that Distance Matters," *Communications of the ACM*, vol. 50, no. 10, 2007, pp. 40–46; E. Carmel and R. Agarwal, "Tactical Approaches for Alleviating Distance in Global Software Development," *IEEE Software*, Mar./Apr. 2001, pp. 22–29; E. Carmel and P. Tjia, *Offshoring Information Technology: Sourcing and Outsourcing to a Global Workforce*, Cambridge University Press, 2005; Lacity and Hirschheim, 1993; M. Lacity and L. Willcocks, *Global Information Technology Outsourcing: Search for Business Advantage*, Wiley, 2001; Lacity and Rottman, 2008; and J. Rottman, "Successfully Outsourcing Embedded Software Development," *Computer*, vol. 39, no. 1, 2006, pp. 55–61.

outsourcing founders, senior executives, delivery center managers, and clients (see Table A1).

For client interviews, we asked questions about their reasons for or drivers of outsourcing, reasons for selecting the rural/impact outsourcing provider, the transition period, the quality of services received, the costs incurred, and lessons learned. For provider interviews, we asked questions about the history of the company; growth of the company in terms of sales and employees; the financials of the companies; current and future competitive positioning; reasons for choosing the delivery center locations; core capabilities in terms of their service offerings; current and past clients; employee recruitment, development, and retention; and lessons learned. All US provider interviews were conducted face-to-face at provider sites. Client interviews were conducted either by phone or face-to-face. In addition to formal interviews, we learned about rural outsourcing from three clients presenting at a conference at which we were also presenters. We also observed and met many more people during visits to providers' training facilities. In our international research, we have thus far focused on RDL provider interviews and site visits. We've completed two site visits to Israeli RDL providers, three interviews with Chinese RDL providers, and three interviews with Indian RDL providers—all located outside the main ITO or BPO centers.

Table A1. Companies Studied				
Firms Studied	**Country**	**Number of Employees in 2010–11**	**Supplier/ Client**	**Number of Interviews**
CrossUSA	US	110	Provider	15
Rural Sourcing, Inc.	US	100	Provider	6
Onshore Outsourcing	US	100	Provider	9
Cayuse Technologies	US	280	Provider	8
Systems in Motion	US	130	Provider	5
Rural America Onshore Outsourcing	US	600	Provider	1
Samasource	US	15	Provider (non-profit)	1
East Coast Healthcare	US	5400	Client	1
Midwest Healthcare 1	US	600	Client	1
Midwest Healthcare 2	US	4200	Client	1
Midwest Legal	US	650	Client	1
Midwest Utility	US	9500	Client	1
Midwest Financial Services	US	5500	Client	2
East Coast Software	US	400	Client	1
Matrix	Israel	500	Provider	1
Galil	Israel	120	Provider	1
HOV Services	India	12,000	Provider	1
Zensar Technologies	India	5,350	Provider	2
Sihong*	China	n/a	Provider	1
Guilin*	China	n/a	Provider	1
Nanchong*	China	n/a	Provider	1
Missouri Partnership	US	n/a	Economic Development	1
			Total:	**62**

* All three Chinese firms are denoted by their cities as pseudonyms.

Appendix B:
Voice of the CEO

Monty Hamilton,
CEO of Rural Sourcing, Inc.

In looking over the past few years, how have your business services or business model evolved in reaction to your customers' needs?

Rural Sourcing's business services have evolved to include practice areas that I never envisioned three years ago. For example, we are providing several leading CPG companies with ongoing support and maintenance in the CRM and Trade Promotions area. This area is a niche for a couple of leading software providers where there are very few, if any, skills located offshore, and the domain knowledge in this area is highly specific to their US business practices between manufacturer and retailer. A second example is in the Identity and Access Management (IAM) area. Our clients in this practice area have been struggling to find and retain talent abroad.

As for the business model, we began to see in mid-2011 significantly larger business opportunities than in my first two years with Rural

Sourcing. I believe that this swing is due to three primary drivers: (1) greater exposure and belief from the buyers in the model itself—many of our buyers are moving from the test-driving stage to full-blown ownership; (2) maturing of the service capabilities—now that a number of the providers have been in the business for three years or more, they have all moved up the capabilities curve in their selected practice areas; and (3) a growing demand for agile: specific solutions delivered via a simpler, less risky delivery model. Our belief is that this trend will continue on a rapid growth curve as we see less and less need for thousands of programmers to convert a mainframe application to a client server technology (economies of scale) and more and more demand for efficient and cost-effective teams providing agile quick-to-market solutions (economies of skill).

Will you please share one short story about an employee's performance that delighted you?

In 2009 when I became CEO of Rural Sourcing, I made the first of many trips to Jonesboro, Arkansas. During the first trip, I was introduced to one of our developers, Amber. Amber hardly looked up from her keyboard during the introduction. Later in the day as I addressed the full team, she lingered way toward the back near the closest exit. On several more occasions within my first three months on board, I tried to engage in conversation with Amber, only to be met with the same quick look of "I am really not comfortable, and can I please get back to programming?" About a year and a half later I was visiting one of our largest clients, a Fortune 500 industrial manufacturer. As we began to discuss RSI's performance and the second phase of work he stopped me and said he'd like to give me some feedback on Amber. Typically when a conversation starts this way with your client, the rest of the conversation is spent with the service provider repeating "Yes, yes, we will look into this" and figuring out how to fix it and ultimately replace them if necessary. However, in this case the client relayed a story that went as follows:

"When Amber first came onto the team, she was hesitant to speak up and reluctant to share her thoughts. However, now our project conversations typically follow the pattern of everyone on our side huddled in my office, including my long-term systems integrator, and my people trying to outwit each other while Amber is on the other end of the phone. Inevitably, someone will ask, 'Amber what do you think?' At which point, everyone else goes quiet and Amber begins to clearly articulate the root cause of the issue, tell us who will handle fixing the problem, and when it will be completed."

Our client went on to say how valuable she had become to the team and how she has become a role model for his own employees. To see this kind of growth in confidence and capability from one of our early hires is truly rewarding and gratifying.

What misconception about rural/impact sourcing would you like to clear up?

At times there is a misconception that people who reside in more rural parts of the United States are less talented or less educated than those in larger, urban cities like New York City and Chicago. The fact of the matter is that the individuals in rural America are just as talented and educated as their urban counterparts; they just choose to live in areas where the quality of life is higher and the cost of living is lower. Now sometimes our colleagues in the Tier 2 and Tier 3 locations can be less verbose in their answers and don't always have the polish and poise of a professional consultant. However, our clients often cite this as a refreshing change from the norm. I often think about the high school quarterback who came from a small rural community in southern California and was not recruited by any four-year schools in the country. In 2002 he enrolled at the local junior college where he led his team to a 10-1 season. Eight years later, after that humble beginning in Butte Junior College, Aaron Rodgers became the MVP of Super Bowl XLV.

Appendix C:
Voice of the CEO

Shane Mayes,
Founder and CEO of Onshore Outsourcing

In looking over the past few years, how have your business services or business models evolved in reaction to your customers' needs?

Onshore was initially focused on our Application Development & Integration, or "build," offering. Over the past few years, we've seen more growth on the "run" side of our business, especially supporting niche activities that are very specific to the client's environment. Clients are more willing to source this type of work to us because of the stability of our rural workforce. Another shift we are seeing is a move away from a remote "staff-augmentation" model toward a "packaged work" or "managed service" model, whereby contracts are structured around the deliverable rather than time spent. Our clients are doing this so that they can do apples-to-apples comparisons between vendors and regions.

Will you please share one short story about an employee's performance that delighted you?

I could give you many stories, but I know you can only pick one. With a passion for technology, David aspired for years to find the career he desired. Despite obtaining an associate's degree in computer programming from a regional trade school, he found himself unemployed and doubting he would ever fulfill his career dreams. Then, through a radio advertisement, David learned about a fifteen-week software development boot camp offered by Onshore. Jumping at the chance, he successfully navigated the required aptitude test and interview process to become enrolled in the intensive, full-time training program. After just two weeks in the boot camp, David admitted the training had already surpassed the skill set provided by his associate's degree. Unfazed, he kept at it and successfully completed the training program. David was later hired at Onshore's Delivery Center in Joplin, Missouri, to perform technology-based services for our clients.

Since joining the company in March 2011, David has served two of Onshore's clients. First, he designed and created Business Objects reports for a large healthcare company based in St. Louis. Now, he performs data extraction and manipulation for a behavioral health-care company based in Dallas. For David, the client work has been both challenging and rewarding. David recently demonstrated his fierce dedication and drive to provide excellent customer service. When faced with a tight deadline due to circumstances beyond his control, David (along with his team leader, Marvin) rolled up their sleeves and made the impossible possible. Over a two-week stretch working long days often into the early morning hours (including one all-nighter), he completed his tasks and made the deadline. Despite his lack of sleep and the long work hours, David maintained a positive attitude through the experience. As a result of his team's efforts, the client recently granted a six-month contract extension. At Onshore, the mission is to give people a hand up and not a hand out. David recently commented, "For the first time in my life I don't dread the alarm clock in the morning. I love what I do, and if not for Onshore I would never have gotten the chance to even try."

What misconception about rural/impact sourcing would you like to clear up?

> Regarding the scalability question... In Macon, Missouri, we have 128,000 working people within a reasonable commute. 95% of the folks would be better off working at Onshore in terms of wages, working conditions, benefits, opportunity for advancement, etc. So I see no reason that we shouldn't be able to scale to 1,000 people between Macon and Joplin, Missouri, and I think that's reasonably scalable. The challenge we must solve is seeding the rural teams with mentors and leaders. To meet this challenge we're building additional capability in an office in St. Louis and rotating rural teams through that office and vice-versa.

Appendix D:
Voice of the CEO

Christopher Chung,
CEO of Missouri Partnership[1]

In looking over the past few years, what policy incentives have you seen which reduce or eliminate start-up costs?

The State of Missouri is continuing to increase its investment in workforce-development incentives, primarily those that assist employers with training new and existing employees. Missouri's New Jobs Training Program and Customized Jobs Training Program are two examples of workforce-centric incentives that complement the state's slate of job-creation tax credits and other assistance for new capital investment projects. While training incentives do not directly address "start-up" costs, they are aimed at ensuring that employers in Missouri can hire and develop talent that will con-

---

1   The Missouri Partnership is a non-profit economic development organization working with other organizations at the state, regional, and local levels to attract new business to the State of Missouri.

tribute to the employer's profitability and success. Additionally, by raising the overall skills of Missouri's workforce, these incentives are indirectly reducing the start-up costs of future new employers, who will spend less time and resources finding qualified employees for their own operations.

Missouri's economic development efforts are also benefiting from stronger partnerships with the higher-education community, specifically by allowing Missouri's two- and four-year colleges and universities to participate in solutions aimed at providing a qualified, skilled workforce. Additionally, the push for increasing telecommunications access in rural parts of the state, as embodied by the "MO Broadband Now" initiative, is helping to reduce infrastructure development costs for companies setting up operations in these communities.

Will you share one short story about a firm that benefited from policies aimed at easing the creation or operations of a rural, impact, or low-cost domestic sourcing firm?

The decision by IBM in 2010 to locate a new IT service-delivery center in Columbia, Missouri, is one of the best examples. Before deciding to locate this new operation in Columbia, home of the University of Missouri's main campus, IBM conducted extensive due-diligence on the availability, cost, and quality of IT workers in mid-Missouri. Previous facility decisions by IBM had looked more closely at real estate and tax factors, rather than on human capital factors; these situations led IBM to spend significantly more time and resources in finding and hiring a qualified workforce, and the company wanted to avoid a similar outcome with its Columbia facility, where it planned to hire 600 direct employees and another 200 contract positions. In addition to benefiting from traditional incentives awarding the company with tax incentives for new job creation and capital investment, IBM also received significant assistance with new employee training through the state's training incentive programs. The University of Missouri at Columbia, Moberly Area Community College, and Linn State Technical College were also all involved as partners in helping the company devise a "pipeline" solution for future hires from IT-related educational disciplines.

Please describe the portfolio of policy incentives your state supports.

Missouri's economic development incentives include refundable/ sellable tax credits based on new job-creation (i.e., as a percentage of new payroll); refundable/sellable tax credits based on new capital investment; new and existing employee training funds; infrastructure-development grants to local communities; and targeted sales tax exemptions for certain types of new facility investment. At the local level, individual communities are also able to waive or abate property taxes owed by a company for real property (e.g., land and buildings) and personal property (e.g., machinery, equipment, furniture, and fixtures). Certain local communities also have loan and grant funds available to new and existing employers.

From an economic development perspective, what is the outlook for the growth areas for ITO and BPO markets in rural America?

As more companies look to diversify their outsourcing alternatives, location options in the rural US make perfect sense as a hedge against the offshore outsourcing risks like rising wages in developing markets, currency fluctuations, quality control, and cross-cultural interaction. This is why US states like Missouri have made "rural sourcing," "farm-shoring," and similar approaches a key part of their strategic plans for economic development. While still a specialized phenomenon within the broader trend of outsourcing, the idea of companies having outsourced functions performed from a near-shore or domestic location bodes well for much of rural America, which, like much of Missouri, is characterized by low business costs, including wages, real estate, taxes, and energy costs. The increasing accessibility of rural America to high-quality Internet and telecommunications infrastructure further strengthens the value proposition that these communities can offer to outsourcing service providers in the ITO and BPO segments.

About the Authors

Dr. Mary Lacity is Curators' Professor of Information Systems at the University of Missouri-St. Louis. She is also Co-chair of the IAOP Midwest Chapter; Industry Advisor for the Outsourcing Angels and the Everest Group; Research Fellow at The Outsourcing Unit, London School of Economics; Coeditor of the Palgrave Series Work, Technology, and Globalization; and on the editorial boards for *Journal of Information Technology, MIS Quarterly Executive, Journal of Strategic Information Systems*, and *Strategic Outsourcing: An International Journal*. She has published 14 books and over 100 academic and practitioner papers.

Dr. Joseph Rottman is the Director of the International Business Institute, an Associate Professor of Information Systems, and a Research Fellow in the Center for International Studies at the University of Missouri-St. Louis. He has conducted case studies in over 40 firms and has been engaged by Fortune 500 firms to analyze their offshore strategies. His recent book *Offshore Outsourcing of IT Work* (with Mary C. Lacity) details models and practices IT professionals can utilize to effectively engage offshore suppliers and explores emerging outsourcing markets such as rural sourcing and the Chinese market. His publications have appeared in *Sloan Management Review, MIS Quarterly Executive, Information Systems Frontiers, Strategic Outsourcing: An International Journal, Computer, Journal of Information Technology, American Review of Public Administration,* and *Information and Management* as well as in leading practitioner outlets such as *CIO Insight* and the *Cutter Consortium.* He was a Research Fellow with the Chinese Academy of Social Sciences in 2009, received the 2006 Anheuser-Busch Excellence in Teaching award, and is on the editorial board of *MIS Quarterly Executive.*

Prof. Erran Carmel's area of expertise is globalization of technology work. He studies global software teams, offshoring of information technology, and emergence of software industries around the world. His 1999 book *Global Software Teams* was the first on this topic and is considered a landmark in the field. He followed this with *Offshoring Information Technology* (2005) and *I'm Working While They're Sleeping* (2011). He has written over 90 articles, reports, and manuscripts. He consults and speaks to industry and professional groups around the world. He is a full professor in American University's department of Information Technology, where he has also served as department chair. In 2009 he was also appointed the International Business Research Professor. In the 1990s he cofounded and led the program in Management of Global Information Technology. He has been a Visiting Professor at University of Haifa (Israel) and University College Dublin (Ireland).

References

J. Arora, "The Risky Side of Offshore Growth: Operational Challenges with Indian Majors?," Everest Research Institute, blog, 25 May 2011, http://www.everestgrp.com/2011-05-the-risky-side-of-offshore-growth-operational-challenges-with-indian-majors-sherpas-in-blue-shirts-4987.html.

R. Babin and B. Nicholson, "Corporate Social and Environmental Responsibility and Global IT Outsourcing," *MIS Quarterly Executive*, vol. 8, no. 4, 2009.

V. Barret, "Silicon Valley's Prison Call Center," *Forbes*, 28 June 2010.

E. Carmel and P. Abbot, "Why Nearshore Means that Distance Matters," *Communications of the ACM*, vol. 50, no. 10, 2007, pp. 40–46.

E. Carmel and R. Agarwal, "Tactical Approaches for Alleviating Distance in Global Software Development," *IEEE Software*, Mar./Apr. 2001, pp. 22–29.

E. Carmel and P. Tjia, *Offshoring Information Technology: Sourcing and Outsourcing to a Global Workforce*, Cambridge University Press, 2005.

D. Carroll, "Behind the Fences: UNICOR's Affect on Private Business," *Business Credit*, vol. 112, no. 3, Mar. 2010, pp. 12–13.

N. Conan, "Inmates' Jobs, From Call Centers to Paint Mixing," *Talk of the Nation*, National Public Radio, broadcast, 16 Dec. 2010.

A. Gruber, "Competing with Inmates," *Government Executive*, vol. 37, no. 12, 2005, pp. 32–34.

R. Hirschheim and M. Lacity, "Information Technology Insourcing: Myths and Realities," *Communications of the ACM*, vol. 43, no. 2, 2000, pp. 99–108.

N. James, *Federal Prison Industries (RL32380)*, Congressional Research Service, 2007, http://digitalcommons.ilr.cornell.edu/key_workplace/309/.

Job Creation Through Building the Field of Impact Sourcing, working paper, Monitor Group and Rockefeller Foundation, 2011, http://www.rockefellerfoundation.org/news/publications/job-creation-through-building-field.

A. Khalfan, "Information security considerations in IS/IT outsourcing projects: a descriptive case study of two sectors," *International Journal of Information Management*, vol. 24, no. 1, 2004, pp. 29–42.

A. Kramer, "Companies Take Call Centers to Prisons Rather than Overseas," *InformationWeek*, 24 Feb. 2004, http://www.informationweek.com/companies-take-call-centers-to-prisons-r/18200370.

M. Lacity and J. Rottman, *Offshore Outsourcing of IT Work*, Palgrave, 2008.

M. Lacity and L. Willcocks, *Global Information Technology Outsourcing: Search for Business Advantage*, Wiley, 2001.

M. Lacity and L. Willcocks, *Advanced Outsourcing Practice: Rethinking ITO, BPO, and Cloud Services*, Palgrave, 2012.

M. Lacity and R. Hirschheim, *Information Systems Outsourcing: Myths, Metaphors and Realities*, Wiley, 1993.

M. Lacity, E. Carmel, and J. Rottman, "Rural Outsourcing: Delivering ITO and BPO Services from Remote Domestic Locations," *Computer*, vol. 44, no. 12, Dec. 2011, pp. 55–62.

M. Lacity, J. Rottman, and S. Khan, "Field of Dreams: Building IT Capabilities in Rural America," *Strategic Outsourcing: An International Journal*, vol. 3, no. 3, 2010, pp. 169–191.

K. Parakala, "Rural BPOs in India: Are they Over-Hyped?," 2011, http://www.globalservicesmedia.com/Experts/Home/Rural-BPOs-in-India:-Are-they-Over-Hyped/30/27/0/GS110309159353.

M.T. Rao, W. Poole, P.V. Raven, and D.L. Lockwood, "Trends, Implications, and Responses to Global IT Sourcing: A Field Study," *Journal of Global Information Technology Management*, vol. 9, no. 3, 2006, pp. 5–23.

J. Rottman, "Successfully Outsourcing Embedded Software Development," *Computer,* vol. 39, no. 1, 2006, pp. 55–61.

J. Rottman, "Successful Knowledge Transfer Within Offshore Supplier Networks: A Case Study Exploring Social Capital In Strategic Alliances," *Journal of Information Technology,* vol. 23, 2008, pp. 31–43.

N. Sandler, "Israel's Matrix Taps Devout Women for IT," *BusinessWeek,* 2009, http://www.businessweek.com/globalbiz/content/sep2009/gb20090916_846021.htm.

C. Saunders, M. Gebelt, and Q. Hu, "Achieving success in information systems outsourcing," *California Management Review,* vol. 39, no. 2, 1997, pp. 63–80.

W. Saylor and G. Gaes, "Training Inmates through industry work participation and vocational and apprenticeship instruction," *Corrections Management Quarterly,* vol. 1, no. 2, 1997, pp. 32–43.

W. Saylor and G. Gaes, "The Differential Effect of Industries and Vocational Training on Post Release Outcomes for Ethnic and Racial Groups," *Corrections Management Quarterly,* vol. 5, no. 4, 2001, pp. 17–24.

F. Sen and M. Shiel, "From Business Process Outsourcing to Knowledge Process Outsourcing: Some Issues," *Human Systems Management,* vol. 25, 2006, pp. 145–155.

G. Smith-Ingley and M. Cochran, "Ruinous or Fair Competition: The Correctional Industries Public Debate," *Corrections Today,* Oct. 1999, pp. 82–100.

D. Straub, P. Weill, and K. Schwaig, "Strategic Dependence on the IT Resource and Outsourcing: A Test of the Strategic Control Model," *Information Systems Frontiers,* vol. 10, no. 2, 2008, pp. 195–211.

J. Teng, M. Cheon, and V. Grover, "Decisions to Outsource Information Systems Functions: Testing a Strategy-Theoretic Discrepancy Model," *Decision Sciences,* vol. 26, no. 1, 1995, pp. 75–103.

E. Walden, "Intellectual Property Rights and Cannibalization in Information Technology Outsourcing Contracts," *MIS Quarterly,* vol. 29, no. 4, 2005, pp. 699–721.

O. Williamson, "Strategizing, Economizing, and Economic Organization," *Strategic Management Journal,* vol. 12, 1991, pp. 75–94.

O. Williamson, "Comparative Economic Organization: The Analysis of Discrete Structural Alternatives," *Administrative Science Quarterly,* vol. 36, no. 2, 1991, pp. 269–296.

M. Zouhali-Worrall, "An Internet for Rural India," CNNmoney.com, 2009, http://money.cnn.com/2009/07/08/smallbusiness/internet_for_india.fsb/index.htm.